First World War
and Army of Occupation
War Diary
France, Belgium and Germany

41 DIVISION
123 Infantry Brigade
Queen's (Royal West Surrey Regiment)
10th Battalion
1 March 1919 - 30 September 1919

WO95/2638/3

The Naval & Military Press Ltd
www.nmarchive.com
Published in association with The National Archives

Published by

The Naval & Military Press Ltd

Unit 10 Ridgewood Industrial Park,

Uckfield, East Sussex,

TN22 5QE England

Tel: +44 (0) 1825 749494

www.naval-military-press.com

www.nmarchive.com

This diary has been reprinted in facsimile from the original. Any imperfections are inevitably reproduced and the quality may fall short of modern type and cartographic standards.

© **Crown Copyright**
Images reproduced by permission of The National Archives, London, England, 2015.

Contents

Document type	Place/Title	Date From	Date To
Heading	WO95/2638/4 10/Queen's (R.W. Surry) Mar 19-Sept 19		
Heading	London Division (Late 41st Division 123rd Infy Bde 10th Bn Q.R. West Surreys Mar 1919-1919 Sep		
War Diary	Engelskirchen	01/03/1919	23/03/1919
War Diary	Ehreshoven	24/03/1919	31/03/1919
Miscellaneous	Fairless Order	08/03/1919	08/03/1919
War Diary	Ehreshoven Germany	01/04/1919	22/04/1919
War Diary	Ehreshoven	21/04/1919	30/04/1919
Miscellaneous	Addition To Operation Order No. 29		
Operation(al) Order(s)	10th Bn. "Queens" Operation Order No. 29	23/04/1919	23/04/1919
Operation(al) Order(s)	Administrative Order To Accompany Operation Order No. 29	28/04/1919	28/04/1919
War Diary	Lindlar Germany	01/05/1919	17/05/1919
War Diary	Lindlar	18/05/1919	28/05/1919
War Diary	Engelskirchen	29/05/1919	31/05/1919
War Diary	(Germany) Engelskirchen	01/06/1919	09/06/1919
War Diary	Engelskirchen	09/06/1919	16/07/1919
War Diary	Engelskirchen And Bensberg	17/07/1919	17/07/1919
War Diary	Bensberg	18/07/1919	17/08/1919
War Diary	Germany	18/08/1919	26/08/1919
War Diary	Bensberg	27/08/1919	27/08/1919
War Diary	Germany	28/08/1919	31/08/1919
Operation(al) Order(s)	10th. Bn. "The Queens" R.W.S. Regiment. Operation Order No. 34.	29/08/1919	29/08/1919
Miscellaneous	1st. Amendment To Administrative Instructions. issued with Operation Order No. 34.	30/08/1919	30/08/1919
Operation(al) Order(s)	1st Amendment To Operation Order No. 38	30/08/1919	30/08/1919
War Diary	Forest Camp Seigburg Germany.	01/09/1919	07/09/1919
War Diary	Forest Camp Seigburg	08/09/1919	30/09/1919
Heading	41st Division 123rd Infy Bde 11th Bn Queen's R.W. Surreys May 1916 Oct 1917		

WO95/2638 (4)
10/Queen's (R.W.Surrey)
Mar '19 - Sept '19

LONDON DIVISION
(LATE 41ST DIVISION)
123RD INFY BDE

10TH BN Q.R. WEST SURREYS
MAR 1919-FEB 1920

1919 SEP

FROM 124 BDE

TO 1 RHINE BDE
RHINE GARRISON

Army Form C. 2118.

10th Bn QUEENS R.W. Surrey Regt. WAR DIARY
or
INTELLIGENCE SUMMARY.
(Erase heading not required.)

MARCH 1919.

Instructions regarding War Diaries and Intelligence Summaries are contained in F. S. Regs., Part II. and the Staff Manual respectively. Title pages will be prepared in manuscript.

Place	Date	Hour	Summary of Events and Information	Remarks and references to Appendices
ENGLESHOVEN	March 1		Battalion in Outpost line Forward Right Sub-Sector. 3 Coys in Outpost duty.	S.n.o
	2		Battalion Church Parade.	S.n.o
	3/8		General training for all Coys. Recreational training and short educational classes. General Idleness.	
	9		Church Parade no rum. Battalion football match a Funeral	S.n.o
	10/15		Training in Musketry Lewis Guns Pt. & Pl. Arms Drill	S.n.o
			P.T. in afternoon. Football Cross-country runs, Room & Rooker Ball	Sng
	16		Church Parade. Bn football match	S.n.o
	17			S.n.o
	18		Cross country runs each Coy. Battalion cross-country run.	
			Battalion school ... Officers	S.n.o
			At 26.00 hours marched to ENGLESHOVEN. Three conferences of 4 OOPs one an hour at 5PM R.M.A. R.H.Q. at ENGLESHOVEN.	
	19/5		Church parade usual Bus. oof. Noting on Publ House held licence.	S.n.o
			Coy contain Armorer lectures on army system of defence.	S.n.o
	23.		Church Parade to Huis oof. Cup tie Drill competition	
			for Brigade Cup. Def: won by A Coy under command of Capt R F de D BERRANGE MC	S.n.o

Army Form C. 2118.

WAR DIARY
or
INTELLIGENCE SUMMARY.
(Erase heading not required.)

Instructions regarding War Diaries and Intelligence Summaries are contained in F.S. Regs., Part II. and the Staff Manual respectively. Title pages will be prepared in manuscript.

Place	Date	Hour	Summary of Events and Information	Remarks and references to Appendices
ELMSHORN	March 29		Units continue working shifts on Rifle Range, interesting time general training and Company drill. Indicator class-cont	
			A and B Coys. Stretcher Bearer class commenced.	
			One company go out on main line of defence.	
			Officers Riding Class held and several Recreational training	Sw
			Company teams training to cross-country run. General sports.	Sw
			Two companies on rifle range. One Coy. general training	
		31	One company on main line of defence	
			Strength at beginning of month.	Strength at end of month
			Reinforcements { 2nd od. 1 Off 3 O.R's Genl. Sect 5 Pt. one parc 11 S.os M Enros 3 4	
			30 Off. 667 O.R's 6 Off. 157 O.R's 4 Off. 23 O.R's	32 Off. 741 O.R's

Sw Watson
Lt. Col.
Commanding 10th Durham R.S. Regt.

FAREWELL ORDER.

The Brigadier General Commanding 124th Infantry Brigade, in saying farewell to all ranks of the 10th Queens Regiment on their transfer to the Queens Brigade in the London Division desires to place on record his appreciation of the gallantry and unfailing success of the Regiment under most trying conditions during the last stages of the Great Campaign to Final Victory, and for the maintenance of their high standard of discipline, efficiency, and esprit de Corps during re-organisation and demobilization since that period.

In thanking all ranks for their gallant and loyal co-operation at all times, he offers his best wishes for continued success.

Brigadier General,
Commanding 124th Infantry Brigade.

Hoffnungsthal
7th March 1919.

Army Form C.

WAR DIARY
or
INTELLIGENCE SUMMARY.

10th Queens

(Erase heading not required.)

Place	Date	Hour	Summary of Events and Information	Remarks and references to Appendices
EHRESHOVEN GERMANY	1/4/19		B Coy routine training and education. A and D Coys working on Lewis Gun Rifle Range. C Coy wiring defences on main line of Resistance at STEFFEN. 51st Grihewald Battalion "The Queen Regt" with Lt Col R.A. Baldwin D.S.O (East Surrey Regt.) in command, and consisting of 41 Officers 755 O.Rs arrived to be absorbed by this Batn.	
	2/4/19		A Coy Routine Training and Education. B + D Coys working on Lewis Gun Rifle Range. C Coy wiring defences at STEFFEN. Farewell letter received from G.O.C. 124 Inf. Bde. Copy attached.	
	3/4/19		A and B Coys working on Rifle Range. C Coy working on defences VILKERATH. D Coy routine training and education. Provisional Defence Scheme drawn up. Copy attached.	
	4/4/19		A and D Coys working on Rifle Range. B Coy Routine Training C Coy wiring defences STEFFEN.	

Army Form C.

WAR DIARY
or
INTELLIGENCE SUMMARY.
(Erase heading not required.)

Place	Date	Hour	Summary of Events and Information	Remarks and references to Appendices
EHRESHOVEN GERMANY.	5/4/19		A and D Coys routine training and education. B Coy working on Rifle Range. C Coy wiring defences STEFFEN	
	6/4/19		Church Parade. Service in KAISERSHAUS LOOPE followed by C.O's inspection.	
	7/4/19		B Coy routine training. A and D Coys working on Rifle Range. C Coy wiring defences at STEFFEN. Lt Col G.H. SAWYER DSO (Royal Berkshire Regt) arrived and took over command of the Battn. Football match for "Inter Coy Challenge Cup" C V A Coy	R Sho Lector GC Circle F 10/5/18 - 1/4 Queen 21.
	8/4/19		A Coy working on Rifle Range. B Coy routine training. C Coy erecting PILL BOXES on main line of Resistance. D Coy two platoons on Rifle Range. Two platoons training. Lt Col S.T. Welsh DSO. "Queens Regt" left to take command of 2/4th "Queens"	
	9/4/19		A B D Coys Routine Training on Rifle Range. C Coy working on Rifle Range.	

WAR DIARY
or
INTELLIGENCE SUMMARY.
(Erase heading not required.)

Army Form C.2118

Instructions regarding War Diaries and Intelligence Summaries are contained in F.S. Regs., Part II. and the Staff Manual respectively. Title pages will be prepared in manuscript.

Place	Date	Hour	Summary of Events and Information	Remarks and references to Appendices
EHRESHOVEN GERMANY	19/4/19		Bn. confirmed on Routine and Practical training for	
"	19/4/19	09.00 to 12.30	H.C.W. training B.Coy fatigue on Disk Range 09.00 to 12.30	
"	19/4/19		Church Parade.	
"	19/4/19		B & C Coys training fatigue & Electrical A Coy Range fatigue 09.00 to 12.30	
"			Nudir new Nomenclature Bath. Arms into British Army A	Robert Leahy Lt Col Cmd 16 = 73 = 76 Que. R4.
"			the Rhine	
"			General fatigue & Electric training carried out by all Coys	
"	21/4/19		Lingual class started	
"	21/4/19		Ditto	
"			Ditto	
"			Bon by Coys to Meuse test Platoon in Luth	
"			Men by Coys to 14 Rifles A Coy	
"			Routine training Signal Class Church Parade billed	
"	23/4/19		Good Friday	
"	23/4/19		General Routine Training All Coys Lingual Class 9 — 12.30	
"	24/4/19		Church Parade Laun in Kareahaus Loft	

WAR DIARY
INTELLIGENCE SUMMARY
(Erase heading not required.)

Army Form C. 2118.

Place	Date	Hour	Summary of Events and Information	Remarks and references to Appendices
Crowborough	2/4/16		Church Parade	
"	23/4/16		Instruction of Scouts 09.00-12.30. Church 11.00-12" Lectures by Divisional Commander	
"	24/4/16		B. Coy. Inspection by C.O. — Organisation B Coy 3 plns. Routine training 09.00-12.30 Inf. Class & Sig. Class 09.00-12.30	
"	25/4/16		Inspection of Batt HQ by CO. All Coys & Specialist classes their routine training	
"	26/4/16		All Companies Routine training	
"	27/4/16		Church Parade Coy arrangements	
"	28/4/16		Training with masks on	
"	29/4/16		Batt relieved 11th Bn Queens Rn Lacey Rfn Bell left under 2nd Lieuttles copy of CO attached	

Robert Lacey C.C. CRU 16-13 V.L. Dec. 16 (upside down at top)

ADDITION TO OPERATION ORDER No. 29.

"D" Coy. will detail a guard to relieve Battalion Quarter Guard of 11th. Bn."Queens" on arrival at LINDLAR.

2/Lieut. A.W.R.Walker will carry the Colours.

O.C. "B" and "D" Coys. will each detail 2 Sergeants and one man to report to 2/Lieut. A.W.R.Walker at Bn.H.Q.Mess by 08.30 hrs. as Colour Escort. On arrival at Lindlar the Colours will be established at Bn.H.Q.Mess.

SECRET.   COPY NO. ......

10th. Bn. "QUEENS" OPERATION ORDER NO. 22.

Map reference - LINNAR - ENGELSKIRCHEN and OVERATH
1: 75,000.

----

1. **INTRODUCTION.**

   Inter-Battalion reliefs will take place as follows on April 30th. 1919.

   2/4th. "Queens" will relieve 10th. "Queens" at ENGELSKIRCHEN.

   10th. Bn. "Queens" will relieve 11th. Bn. "Queens" in the Left Sector of the Outpost Line.

   11th. Bn. "Queens" will relieve 2/4th. Bn. "Queens" in the Right Sector of the Outpost Line.

2. **INTENTION.**

   The Battalion will move from present area and will relieve 11th. Bn. "Queens" in the Left Sector of the Outpost Line.

3. **INSTRUCTIONS.**

   The Battalion will proceed by march route as follows :-
   Bn.H.Q., "A" Coy, "B" Coy. and "D" Coy. via LOOPE, ENGELSKIRCHEN and LINNAR.
   "C" Coy. via UNTER VILKERATH, RONKARST. and LINNAR.

   Starting Point for Bn.H.Q., "A", "B" and "D" Coys. will be "D" Coy. H.Qrs. C. 44.45.
   Head of column to pass Starting Point at 09.00 hrs.
   "C" Coy. will leave VILKERATH at 08.30 hrs.

   Distances of 10 yards between platoons and 100 yards between companies will be maintained.

   ORDER OF MARCH. Drums - Bn.H.Q. - "D" Coy. - "B" Coy. - "A" Coy. - Transport.

   "A" Coy. will relieve "B" Coy. 11th. "Queens" in the Right Sub-Sector as follows :-

No. 1 Post.	HORPE	N. 73.93.	½ platoon.
No. 2 Post.	ENGER	N. 75.03.	½ platoon.
No. 3 Post.	KAISTRAH	N.87.04.	½ platoon.
No. 4 Post.	EQUIEL.	N. 94.26.	1 platoon.

   Company Headquarters and 1½ platoons in MIELENBORN.

   "C" Coy. will relieve "C" Coy. 11th. Bn. "Queens" in the Left Sub-Sector with one platoon in each of the following posts :-

No. 5 Post.	about N. 80.44.
No. 6 Post.	N. 85.51.
No. 7 Post.	Ober Buschem N. 81.63.
No. 8 Post.	Ober Steinbach. N. 75.80.

   Company Headquarters in WIRTZCARTH.

/ see over.

(2)

"B" Coy. will relieve "A" Coy. 11th. "Queens" at LINDLAR.

"D" Coy. will relieve "DUMMY "C" Coy. 11th. "Queens" at LINDLAR.

Guides from 11th. "Queens" will meet "A" Coy. at H. 88.89 at 1000 hrs., "C" Coy. at the Church, LINDLAR at 10.00 hrs. and H.Q. "B" and "D" Coys. at the entrance to the village at 10.00 hrs.

Advance parties of one N.C.O. and two men per post will be sent on to each administrative post 24 hours in advance.

Billeting parties of 1 officer and two N.C.O's per company and 1 officer and two N.CO's per Bn.H.Q. will also be sent on 24 hours in advance.

These parties will carry rations for the 24 hours.

All posts, defence schemes, orders and area stores will be carefully taken and handed over, and receipts given and obtained.

During the relief of each post an officer of both incoming and outgoing Battalions will be present.

Completion of relief will be notified by wire to Orderly Room as soon as possible.

2/4th. "Queens" will take over the present billets of this Battalion from opposite numbers. Billeting parties will arrive 24 hours in advance.

Administrative Orders attached.

ACKNOWLEDGE

V.R.Gilbert.
2/Lieut. & A/Adjt.
10th. Bn. "Queens" R.W.S.Regt.

A   Issued at ....hrs. 25.4.19.

     Copies to -   No. 1.   Commanding Officer
                  2.   Second in Command.
                  3.   Adjutant.
                  4.   Bde.
                  5.   War Diary.
                  6.   O.C. Bn.H.Q.
                  7.   O.C. "A" Coy.
                  8.   O.C. "B" Coy.
                  9.   O.C. "C" Coy.
                 10.   O.C. "D" Coy.
                 11.   Quartermaster
                 12.   Transport Officer.
                 13.   2nd. London Bde.
                 14.   11th. "Queens"
                 15.   2/4th. "Queens"
                 16.   Spare.

ADMINISTRATIVE ORDERS TO ACCOMPANY
OPERATION ORDER NO. 29.

1. Blankets, Stores, Officers' and men's kits will be dumped outside each Company H.Q. before moving off.
Bn.H.Q.Stores and Orderly Room boxes will be dumped outside Q.M.Stores by 07.30.hrs. Q.M. and T.O. will arrange to collect.

One G.S. wagon will be at "C" Coy. H.Q. by 07.30 hrs to pick up officers' kits, Mess baskets and dixies. This will move with company and will be returned to LINDLAR immediately it is un-loaded.

One limber will report to "A" Coy.; one to "B" Coy. and one to "D" Coy. H.Q. at 07.30 hrs. to carry mess baskets, dixies and unconsumed portion of the day's rations. These limbers will march with Transport."A" Coy. limber will join Coy. when it leaves the column at N. 68.69., and return to LINDLAR after unloading.

Lewis Gun limbers of "A" "B" and "D" Coy. will march with Transport. "A" Coy. limber will join company when it leaves the column.
"C" Coy. L.G. limber will move with company.

2. Each company will detail 1 N.C.O. and 10 men to remain at Company Lines as guard and loading party.
R.S.M. will detail 20 men from B.H.Q. to report to Quartermaster at 07.30 as loading party.

3. All billets, messes, recreation rooms, latrines etc. will be handed over in a clean and sanitary condition.
Certificates will be obtained from civilians that no unnecessary damage has been caused to billets etc. occupied.
The usual billet certificates will be rendered to Orderly Room.

4. All Timber, Canvas, Latrine buckets, etc. will be handed over as area stores.
25 bell tents will be taken over from 11th. "Queens".

F.N.Gilbert
2/Lieut. A A/Adjt.
10th. Bn."Queens" R.E.Surrey Regt.

29.4.19.

Copy to all recipients of Operation Order No. 29.

Army Form C. 2118.

WAR DIARY
or
INTELLIGENCE SUMMARY.
(Erase heading not required.)

Instructions regarding War Diaries and Intelligence Summaries are contained in F. S. Regs., Part II. and the Staff Manual respectively. Title pages will be prepared in manuscript.

10th Queen's

Place	Date	Hour	Summary of Events and Information	Remarks and references to Appendices
LINDLAR GERMANY.	1/5/19		A & C Coys Outpost Duty. B Coy Combat Training. B Coy wiring train	
			Line of Resistance KEMMERICH - VILLENGEN	
	2/5/19		A & C Coy Outposts. B Combat Training D Wiring as above	
	3/5/19		ditto ditto B " "	
			D Coy Route march	
	4/5/19		Church Parades B & D Coys & BHQ C of E KAISERSHALL LINDLAR	
			R C's C Church LINDLAR. 120 men left for attachment to various	
			Arms of the Service	
	5/5/19		A & C Coy's. Outposts. D Coy Combat Training. Education classes started	
			for Junior N.C.O's (General) Lewis Gunners, Scouts, Stretcher Bearers.	
			B Coy Wiring KEMMERICH	
	6/5/19		A & C Outposts. B Coy Firing on Range at EHRESHOVEN. D Wiring	
			Education for all Companies 07.00 - 08.00 and 17.00 - 18.00.	
	7/5/19		A & C Outpost Duty. D Coy Combat Training. B Coy Wiring KEMMERICH.	
			Education as above. No 14 Platoon 9 Coy Competed for their Bde Competition for Drill etc	
	8/5/19		BHQ Parade for Inspection under 2/Lt P Harwood. A & C Coys Outpost Duty	
			B Coy Route March. D Coy wiring - KEMMERICH. Education as above.	

Army Form C. 2118.

WAR DIARY
or
INTELLIGENCE SUMMARY.
(Erase heading not required.)

Instructions regarding War Diaries and Intelligence Summaries are contained in F. S. Regs., Part II. and the Staff Manual respectively. Title pages will be prepared in manuscript.

Place	Date	Hour	Summary of Events and Information	Remarks and references to Appendices
LINDLAR GERMANY	9/5/19		A & B Coys Outpost Duty, 9 Coy Routine Training. B Coy wiring KEMMERICH. Education for all Coys 07.00 – 08.00 and 17.00 – 18.00	
ditto	10/5/19		A & C Coys Outpost Duty. B Coy Routine Training. D Coy Scheme (Outposts).	
ditto	11/5/19		A & C Coys Outpost duty. Church Parade B & D Coys & H.Q.	
			C of E in KAISERSHALL – LINDLAR. RC's Church Lindlar. Conference of Company Commanders. B.H.Qrs.	
ditto	12/5/19		A & C Coys Outpost Line. B Coy wiring tram line Residence. Hon. Inspection by Commanding Officer.	
"	13/5/19		A & C Coys Outpost Duty. B & D Coys Routine Training & Education.	
"	14/5/19		B & D Companies relieved A & C in Outpost Line. Working Orders attached.	
"	15/5/19		A Coy Training – C Coy wiring tram line Residence. B & D Outposts.	
"	16/5/19		Lecture to A & C Coys on "British Character Builders" by Ven. Archdeacon Jones. Officers Riding Class started.	
"	17/5/19		C Coy Routine Training & Education. A Coy Wiring. B & D Outposts. Inspection by Corps Commander, of A & C Companies.	

WAR DIARY
or
INTELLIGENCE SUMMARY.
(Erase heading not required.)

Army Form C. 2118.

Place	Date	Hour	Summary of Events and Information	Remarks and references to Appendices
Lindlar	18/5/19		Church Parade. C of E in KAISERSHALL 11.15 R.C. Lindlar Church 1100	
	19/5/19		Conference Coy Commanders 12.00 hours.	
Lille	20/5/19		A & B Coys Routine Training & Education. B&D Outpost duty	
"			A Coy Firing Musketry Course on EHRESHOVEN Range 09-00 -14.00. C Coy Routine Training. B&D Outpost	
"	21/5/19		A Coy Routine Training - C Coy Route March. B&D Outpost	
"	22/5/19		A Coy Routine Training & Tactical Scheme. C Coy Routine Training. B&D Coys Outpost Duty.	
"	23/5/19		A Coy Routine Training & Route March. C Coy Routine Training. B&D Coys Outposts. Conference Coy Comdrs 10.00 hours.	
"	24/5/19		"A" & "C" Coys Routine Training. B&D Coys outpost	
"	25/5/19		Church Parade. C of E in KAISERSHALL R.C. LINDLAR Church.	
"	26/5/19		A & C Coys Routine Training. B & D Coys outpost.	
"	27/5/19		A & C Coys Routine Training. B & D Coys outpost	
"	28/5/19		The Battn moved from LINDLAR to ENGELSKIRCHEN, being relieved in LINDLAR by the 2/4th Queens and relieving the 11th Queens in ENGELSKIRCHEN on	

WAR DIARY
or
INTELLIGENCE SUMMARY.
(Erase heading not required.)

Army Form C. 2118.

Place	Date	Hour	Summary of Events and Information	Remarks and references to Appendices
	28.5.19		Completed of relief dispositions were as follows:-	
			B'Hq, "B" and "D" Coys in ENGELSKIRCHEN	
			"C" Coy on outpost with Coy Hq and 2 platoons in ENGELSKIRCHEN	
			"A" " " " " HARDT.	
ENGELSKIRCHEN	29.5.19		"A" & "C" Coy on outpost. "B" and "D" Coy at disposal of Coy. Commanders.	
"	30.5.19		"A" & "C" Coy on outpost "B" and "D" Coys Routine Training	
"	31.5.19		"A" & "C" Coy on outpost. "B" and "D" Coys Routine Training	

STRENGTH 1/5/19		INCREASE		DECREASE		STRENGTH 31/5/19	
OFF	O.Rs.	OFF	ORs	OFF	ORS	OFF	ORs
				DEMOB:-			
					38		
				EVAC? SICK:-			
				19	39		
				OTHER CAUSES:-			
65	1275	-	12	19	47	46	1240

Army Form C. 2118.

WAR DIARY
or
INTELLIGENCE SUMMARY.
(Erase heading not required.)

10th Queen's

Instructions regarding War Diaries and Intelligence Summaries are contained in F. S. Regs., Part II. and the Staff Manual respectively. Title pages will be prepared in manuscript.

Place	Date	Hour	Summary of Events and Information	Remarks and references to Appendices
(Germany)	1.6.19			
ENGELSKIRCHEN			Church Parade:- C of E in Protestant Church ENGELSKIRCHEN at 08.15 hrs. Drums, Band & "D" Coy. attended.	
"	2.6.19		In order to celebrate "The Glorious 1st of June" this was observed as a general holiday for the men. Several Platoon Cricket matches were played. The Batt: Concert Party gave an entertainment in the evening.	
"	3.6.19		This being H.M. The King's birthday a general holiday was observed throughout the Army of the Rhine. All available men turned out at 08.00 hrs in the village and gave "Three cheers for H.M. The King".	C.O. Comd'g 10th B: 9th Decr. '18
"	4.6.19		"A" and "C" Coys. on outpost. "B" and "D" Coys. Railway Training.	R.W. Lascom Capt 10 B: 9th Dec: '18
"	5.6.19		"A" and "C" " " " "B" "D" " " "	
"	6.6.19		"A" " "C" " " " "B" "D" " "	
"	7.6.19		"A" " "C" " "	
"	8.6.19		Church Parade as follows:- C of E in Protestant Church, ENGELSKIRCHEN at 09.15 hrs. "B" and "D" Coys. with Drums attended; Presbyterian and Free Church in same place at 11.30 hrs.	
"	9.6.19		This being Whit Monday was observed as a holiday. Various	

Army Form C. 2118.

WAR DIARY
or
INTELLIGENCE SUMMARY.
(Erase heading not required.)

Instructions regarding War Diaries and Intelligence Summaries are contained in F. S. Regs., Part II. and the Staff Manual respectively. Title pages will be prepared in manuscript.

Place	Date	Hour	Summary of Events and Information	Remarks and references to Appendices
ENGELSKIRCHEN	9.6.19		Games of sport i.e. cricket, shooting and swimming were indulged in	
"	10.6.19		"B" and "D" Coys Routine Training. "A" and "C" Coys. outposts.	
"	11.6.19		The following inter-company reliefs took place:-	
			"B" Coy. relieved "A" Coy. in the Right outer sector of the Battn. front	
			"D" " " "C" " " " Left " " " " "	
			On completion of relief Coys were disposed as follows:-	
			"A" and "C" Coys in the camp at ENGELSKIRCHEN	
			"B" Coy. on the Right outpost line with Coy. Hq. at HARDT.	
			"D" " " " Left " " " " " " ENGELSKIRCHEN.	
			Relief was complete by 12.00 hrs.	
"	12-6-19		A & C Coys Routine Training. B & D Coys Outposts.	
"	13-6-19		A & C Coys passed through Gas Chamber, and carried out Routine Training. B & D Coys. Outposts	
"	14-6-19		A and C Coys. relieve two Platoons D Coy. Routine Training. Remainder Outpost Duty.	
"	15-6-19		Church Parade for all Free-Churchmen in ENGELSKIRCHE Protestant Church	11.30 cont. over

WAR DIARY
or
INTELLIGENCE SUMMARY.
(Erase heading not required.)

Army Form C. 2118.

Place	Date	Hour	Summary of Events and Information	Remarks and references to Appendices
ENGELSKIRCHEN	15-6-19		Services for RC's in Catholic Church 11.00	
"	16/6/19		Inspection of A + C Coys, HQrs and Transport by Commander-in-Chief, in YMCA Field 11.15, & afterwards marched past in fours. C in C expressed appreciation of smart turn out of the Bn.	
"	17/6/19		A + C Coys, and 2 Platoons D Coy Routine Training, remainder Outposts. Preparations begin for "Advance" (in case Peace Terms not signed)	copy orders attached
"	18/6/19		Col R.O'H Livesay appointed O.C. Advance Guard	
"	15/6/19		A + C Coys and 2 Platoons D Coy Routine Training. hm of B + C Coys who entered for 2nd class Army Education Certificate attended Exam in the SCHOOL HARDT. Further preparations for advance.	
"	19/6/19		A + C Coys plus 2 platoons D Coy Routine Training & Education. Remainder Outpost duty. Original day to move forward but postponed	13
"	20/6/19		A + C Coys Routine Training and Education. Remainder Outpost duty.	2 C E
"	21/6/19		Church Parade H.of.C. Divine Service in Protestant Church Engelskirchen 10.45 hrs. A + C Coys and Drums attended. RC's Service in Protestant Church 11.00 hrs.	Rev. Lues Rev. 13: H Deere Capt 16: 13: H Deere

Army Form C. 2118.

WAR DIARY
or
INTELLIGENCE SUMMARY.
(Erase heading not required.)

Instructions regarding War Diaries and Intelligence Summaries are contained in F. S. Regs., Part II. and the Staff Manual respectively. Title pages will be prepared in manuscript.

Place	Date	Hour	Summary of Events and Information	Remarks and references to Appendices
ENGELSKIRCHEN	23/6/19		A & C Coys. Routine Training. 2 Platoons D. Coy. Training. Remainder on Outpost duty.	
"	24/6/19		A & C Coys. Routine Training. Inter Platoon relief of D. Coy. Outposts. B. Coy. Outpost Duty.	
"	25/6/19		A & C Coys & 2 Platoons D. — Routine Training. Remainder Outpost Duty.	
"	26/6/19		A & C Coys & 2 Platoons D. Coy. — Routine Training. Remainder Outpost Duty. Bath. Aquatic Sports held in afternoon.	
"	27/6/19		A & C Coys plus two Platoons D. — Routine Training — Remainder Outpost Duty.	
"	28/6/19		A & C Coys & two Platoons D. " " Remainder " "	
"	29/6/19		Church Parades. 6 a/E Divine Service 11.30 in Protestant Church. Engelskirchen attended by A & C Coys. R.C. Holy mass 11.00 in Catholic Church. Presbyterian and Free Church morning Service 12.00 in Protestant Church.	
"	30/6/19		A & C Coys. and 2 Platoons D. Coy Routine Training — Remainder Outpost Duty. Aquatic Sports Finals held.	

Army Form C. 2118.

WAR DIARY
or
INTELLIGENCE SUMMARY.
(Erase heading not required.)

Instructions regarding War Diaries and Intelligence Summaries are contained in F. S. Regs., Part II. and the Staff Manual respectively. Title pages will be prepared in manuscript.

Place	Date	Hour	Summary of Events and Information	Remarks and references to Appendices
ENGELSKIRCHEN	1/7/19		A & C Coys Routine Training - B and D Coys Outpost duty.	
	2/7/19		A Coy relieved B Coy in Right Sub-sector. C Coy relieved D Coy in Left Sub-sector Outpost line.	
	3/7/19		A General Holiday was kept to celebrate the signing of Peace.	
	4/7/19		The Divil Commander Genl Sir S.T.B. LAWFORD KCB Inspected Bn HQrs, B&D Coys and the Transport on parade, afterwards the Coys, A&C on Outpost. Colonel Ro'H Livery left the Baltn to proceed to take Command of a Brigade in England.	
	5/7/19		B & D Coys and 2 platoons C Coy Routine Training. Remainder Outpost duty.	
	6/7/19		Church Parades. Coys Engelskirchen Protestant Church. Divine Service 11.00 hrs. Drums B&D Coys attended R.C. Hly Mass 09.30 hrs - Conformist 10.15 hrs. Protestant Church	
	7/7/19		B & D Coys Company Training. 2 Platoons C Coy Rnline Training. Remainder Outpost duty.	

Army Form C. 2118.

WAR DIARY
or
INTELLIGENCE SUMMARY.
(Erase heading not required.)

Instructions regarding War Diaries and Intelligence Summaries are contained in F. S. Regs., Part II. and the Staff Manual respectively. Title pages will be prepared in manuscript.

Place	Date	Hour	Summary of Events and Information	Remarks and references to Appendices
ENGELSKIRCHEN	8/9/19		Bath. Athletic Sports held in afternoon.	
"	9/9/19		B Coy Tactical Scheme & Route March. D Coy Company Training, two platoons. C Coy Platoon Training, remainder Outpost Duty. Finals Bn. Sports	
"	9/4/19		B & D Coys Company Training. Two platoons C Coy Routine Training. Remainder Outpost Duty.	
"	10/4/19		R Coy. Coy Training. 9 Coy Route March & Scheme. Two platoons C Coy Platoon Training and remainder on Outpost duty.	
"	11/7/19		Demonstration to B & D Coys of Guard mounting from 09.30 – 10.30	
"	12/4/19		B & D Coys Coy Training for remainder of morning. Two platoons of C Coy Routine Training, remainder Outpost duty. B & D Coys and 2 platoons C Coy Routine Training. Athletic Sports of 2 London I.B. Group Competition Cup was won by this Batt.	
"	13/4/19		Church Parade. C of E in Protestant Church at 11.00 hrs. B & D Coys attended. R.C. Holy mass at 10.30 hrs in Catholic Church.	

Army Form C. 2118.

WAR DIARY
or
INTELLIGENCE SUMMARY.
(Erase heading not required.)

Instructions regarding War Diaries and Intelligence Summaries are contained in F. S. Regs., Part II. and the Staff Manual respectively. Title pages will be prepared in manuscript.

Place	Date	Hour	Summary of Events and Information	Remarks and references to Appendices
ENGELSKIRCHEN	14/7/19		B & D Coys Company Training. 2 Platoons E Coy Platoon Training. Remainder on Outpost Duty.	
"	15/7/19		B & D Coys Company Training. Two Platoons of E Coy Continued Trng. Remainder Outpost duty.	
"	16/7/19		B & D Coys Company Training. Two Platoons of E Coy Platoon Training. Remainder Outpost duty.	
do and Bensberg	17/7/19		Battn. relieved by 23rd Bn Middlesex Regt moved to Bensberg by train. Orders for move attached.	
Bensberg	18/7/19		Whole Battn. on Fatigues to clean Barracks.	
"	19/7/19		General Holiday was kept for peace celebration.	
"	20/7/19		Church Parades. C of E Bn paraded on Barrack Square for Divine Service at 09.45 hrs. Non-conformist – morning service in Chapel of Barracks 09.00 hrs. R.C. Holy hed in Catholic Church at 11.15 a.m.	
"	21/7/19		Whole Battn. Carried out Company Training i.e. Schemes.	

Army Form C. 2118.

WAR DIARY
or
INTELLIGENCE SUMMARY.
(Erase heading not required.)

Instructions regarding War Diaries and Intelligence Summaries are contained in F. S. Regs., Part II. and the Staff Manual respectively. Title pages will be prepared in manuscript.

Place	Date	Hour	Summary of Events and Information	Remarks and references to Appendices
Bonberg	22/4/19		Company Training. All Coys carried out Company Drill, Ceremonial, Marching as a Sentry, Saluting without Arms. Education carried out in Evening for one hour.	
"	23/4/19		ditto.	
"	24/4/19		A and D Coys Firing on Range at BRUCK. B & C Coys Section Training and Education. B Coy judged in Inter Coy Drill Competition.	
"	25/4/19		A, B & D Coys judged for Inter Coy Drill competition. A Lewis gun competition was staged. Selected to represent the Bn in Group Competition. A Coy judged for Group Competition. Remainder carried out Company Training. C & D Coys Tactical Scheme.	
"	26/4/19		Church Parade. C. of E. Grand Service 09.30 hrs. Bath formed up on Barrack square and attended the service which was held in a Read Room. Non-Conformist morning service in Schloss Chapel 09.00 hrs. R.C. Bonberg Church 11/15 hrs.	

C.H. Davies (Major)
Comdg. 1st Queens (R & S) R.A.

D. D. & L., London, E.C.
(A8004) Wt. W1771/M12-31 750,000 5/17 Sch. 83 Forms/C2118/14

WAR DIARY
or
INTELLIGENCE SUMMARY.

(Erase heading not required.)

Army Form C. 2118.

Place	Date	Hour	Summary of Events and Information	Remarks and references to Appendices
Bensberg	28/7/19		A and D Coys Company Scheme and Education. B + C Coys Company training from 09.00 - 10.45. 10.45 - 12.45 Education.	
"	29/7/19		B and C Coys Tactical Scheme. A + D Company training.	
"	30/7/19		Batt. Route march for two hours. Route Platz, Miltzfeld, Unter Eschbach, Brudertracel, and back to Bensberg. Education remainder of morning.	
"	31/7/19		B and C Coys Range Practice at Bruck. A + D Coys Company training. Tactical scheme included by Stop.	

G.D. Marsh BM.
Comg. 10th Queens (R.W.S.) Regt.

Army Form C. 2118.

WAR DIARY
or
INTELLIGENCE SUMMARY.
(Erase heading not required.)

Instructions regarding War Diaries and Intelligence Summaries are contained in F. S. Regs., Part II. and the Staff Manual respectively. Title pages will be prepared in manuscript.

Place	Date	Hour	Summary of Events and Information	Remarks and references to Appendices
Bedburg	1/9/19		B Coy Tactical Scheme and Education. Remainder Company Training and Education.	
"	2/9/19		Companies carried out Company Training.	
"	3/9/19		Church Parades C of E divine Services in C&D Coys messroom at 10.30 hrs. Roman Catholic Hy Mass Bedberg Church 11.15hrs. Non-Conformists hearing Service in Bedberg Schloss Chapel 0945.	
"	4/9/19		Companies carried out Company Training. Classes commenced for Senior NCO's, and Provisional Bayonet Fencing.	
"	5/9/19		Coys carried out Tactical Schemes and Education.	
"	6/9/19		Bn Parade was held to Rehearse for Review Rehearsal. "A" Coy carried out Firing on Bruck Range in afternoon. C.O. Inspected Field Kitchens with a view to deciding the one to represent Batn at Divl Trials for Army Hotchkiss Show.	
"	7/9/19		Bn proceeded in Busses to EXERCIER PLATZ NIPPES. C.C.V Corps (less 41st Batn) in Review Rehearsal which was carried out by G.O.C VI Corps.	

Army Form C. 2118.

WAR DIARY
or
INTELLIGENCE SUMMARY.
(Erase heading not required.)

Place	Date	Hour	Summary of Events and Information	Remarks and references to Appendices
Beneberg	8/8/19		All Companies carried out Company Training.	
"	9/8/19		Bde Boys. Company Scheme. A+D Company Drill + Interior Economy.	
"	10/8/19		Church Parades. C of E Divine Service in YMCA Beneberg at 11.15 hrs. 10.00 hrs Roman Catholic Beneberg Church Holy mass 11.15 hrs. Non Conformist morning Service. 09.00 hrs Schloss Chapel.	Kennedy
"	11/8/19		Bn Ceremonial Parade and Education.	
"	12/8/19		Bde Ceremonial Parade on Exerzier Platz K.M.K. 10.00 hrs.	
"	13/8/19		All Companies carried out Company Training and education. NCO's and Provisional B.J. Classes re started C.O. fired on Bryn. Bruch	
"	14/8/19		Companies Carried out Training as for 13th. Bn Rifle meeting was held at Chuloven to select teams for Bde Trials for Lewis Gun and Rifle shooting.	
"	15/8/19		Company Training carried out, including Coy Schemes by B + C Coys.	
"	16/8/19		Company Training was carried out by all Coys. Bde Trials for Lewis Rifle meeting held at Chuloven seven teams took part from NCO's + B.J. Class disposed.	

Lt. Col

Army Form C. 2118.

WAR DIARY
or
INTELLIGENCE SUMMARY.
(Erase heading not required.)

Instructions regarding War Diaries and Intelligence Summaries are contained in F. S. Regs., Part II. and the Staff Manual respectively. Title pages will be prepared in manuscript.

Place	Date	Hour	Summary of Events and Information	Remarks and references to Appendices
Bensberg	17/8/19		Church Parades were held for all denominations as for the 10th August	
Germany	18/8/19		The Battalion in connection with 2nd London F.B. took part in the review held by the Army Council, held on the EXERZIER PLATZ N. of LONGRICH — COLOGNE ending the Infantry in the march past.	
"	19/8/19		A B C D Coys carried out Company Schemes and D. Coy. Routine Training. An Educational detail was held in the evening.	
"	20/8/19		A B & D Companies carried out Company Training & Education. C Coy Range Practice at BRUCK.	
"	21/8/19		Companies carried out Company Training and a Lecture by Lt Bipton Khury on the "West Indies and the Panama Canal" was attended by the Battalion	
"	22/8/19		B C & D Coys carried out Company Training & Education. A Coy Range Practice Bruck.	
"	23/8/19		All Coys. Company Training and Indoor Economy.	
"	24/8/19		Church parades as for Aug 17th	
"	25/8/19		Company Training and Education was carried out by all Companies.	
"	26/8/19		A B & D Coys carried out Tactical Schemes. C Coy Rocket Training. Educational details carried out in evening.	

D. D. & L., London, E.C.
(A8004) Wt. W17171/M231 750,000 5/17 Sch. 52 Forms/C2118/14

Army Form C. 2118.

WAR DIARY
or
INTELLIGENCE SUMMARY.
(Erase heading not required.)

Instructions regarding War Diaries and Intelligence Summaries are contained in F. S. Regs., Part II. and the Staff Manual respectively. Title pages will be prepared in manuscript.

Place	Date	Hour	Summary of Events and Information	Remarks and references to Appendices
Bensberg Germany	27/9/19		All Companies carried out Company Training and Education	
"	28/9/19		ditto	
"	29/9/19		"	
"	30/9/19		All Coys carried out Company Training and Interior Economy.	
"	5/10/19		Church Parades were held. C of E. service in the YMCA at 09.30 hrs. Both less NCO's & OR's attended. Non-Conformist morning service in the Schloss Chapel at 09.00 hrs.	

Signed
Cmdg 1st Queens Regt.

10th. Bn. "The Queens" R.W.S. Regiment.

OPERATION ORDER NO. 34.

1. **INFORMATION.**
    The 2nd. London Infantry Brigade (less 11th. "Queens" and L.T.M. Batty.) will move to the SIEGBURG Area on September 1st. and 2nd, and will take over the Right Battalion Sector of the front lately occupied by the Eastern Division.

2. In connection with the above.-
    (a) The Battalion will move to FOREST CAMP, and from there take over guards now found by the 51st. Bn. Manchester Regiment on September 1st., as under -
    (b) "B" Company will relieve the guard over the Dynamite Factory and Magazines in LIND, North of SIEGBURG. Strength 1 Officer & 70 O.Rks.
    (c) "D" Company will relieve
    1. Railhead Duties at SIEGBURG ... ... 15 O.Ranks.
    2. Army Ammunition Dump, SIEGBURG ... ... 50 O.Ranks.
    3. Geschoss Fabrik, SIEGBURG ... ... 2 sentries
                                    (found from Guard 2 above)
    4. Army Technical College ... ... 6 O.Ranks.
                                    (Regtl. Police)
    5. N.A.C.B Canteen, SIEGBURG ... ... 4 O.Ranks.

    Os.C "B" and "D" Companies will proceed to SIEGBURG on Sunday and meet a guide of 51st. Bn. Manchester Regt., at D.A.P.M's Office SIEGBURG at 15.00 hours, who will show them round the Guards, etc., and inform them of all details concerning the same.

3. Completion of reliefs will be notified to Orderly Room as early as possible.

4. A guard of 4 N.C.Os and 12 men will be left behind at BENSBERG BARRACKS to guard all Area Stores. Personnel for this guard will be provided as under -
    "A" Coy .... 1 Cpl. and 3 men.
    "B" Coy .... 1 Sgt.(i/c Guard) and 3 men.
    "C" Coy .... 1 L/Cpl. and 3 men.
    "D" Coy .... 1 L/Cpl. and 3 Men.

    Instructions for this guard will be issued from Orderly Room.

5. On September 1st. -
    (a) The Battalion will form up on the Barrack Square in close column of Companies, facing the Main Gate,(ready to embus) by 10.15 hours.
    (b) All men on Battalion Headquarters (except Drums and Transport) will rejoin their Companies and will be accomodated with them at FOREST CAMP.
    (c) 30 Busses will be available and these will be allotted before moving. Markings will be A 1, etc., the letter representing the Coy. to which allotted.
    Lieut.C.J. BOYTE will be in charge of Embussing.

6. First Line Transport will proceed by March Route, leaving BENSBERG at 07.30 hours. Mobilization Stores will be carried.

7. **ADVANCE PARTIES.** An Advance Party consisting of -
    1 Officer, Lieut. TRYTHALL
    1 Senior N.C.O. and 3 men per Company.
    1 O.Rank for Transport.
    2 O.Ranks for Bn.H.Qrs (1 Signaller & 1 O.Room Clerk)
    Lewis Gun N.C.O.
    1 Cook, to be detailed by O.C. "A" Coy.

    will proceed by lorry leaving Bn. H.Qrs at 14.00 hours, to-morrow, 30th. inst., and will take over the Range, all Camp Stores, etc., on arrival and will re-arrange accomodation. Details will be issued separately.

/8.

(2)

8. Battalion Headquarters will close at BENSBERG at 10.30 hours, and open at FOREST CAMP at the same hour.

ACKNOWLEDGE.

                (Sgd) F.W. Gilbert,

                    Capt. & Adjt.,
August 29th. 1919.   10th. Bn. "The Queens" R.W.S. Regt.

   Issued at ....

Copies to -
- No. 1 - Commanding Officer.
- 2   Second in Command.
- 3   Adjutant.
- 4   File.
- 5   O.C. 51st. Bn. Manchester Regt.
- 6   2nd. London Infantry Bde. H.Q.
- 7   O.C. "A" Coy.
- 8   O.C. "B" Coy.
- 9   O.C. "C" Coy.
- 10   O.C. "D" Coy.
- 11   Quartermaster.
- 12   Transport Officer.
- 13   Signal Officer (for Bn.H.Qrs)
- 14   Lewis Gun Officer.
- 15   War Diary.
- 16   Town Commandant, Bensberg.
- 17   R.S.M.

1st. Amendment to Administrative Instructions issued with OPERATION ORDER No. 34.

Para. 2.   Cancel and substitute the following :-
Breakfasts will be arranged early.
After breakfast, utensils required for cooking the dinner will be packed on Companies Store Lorry, which will proceed immediately to Forest Camp.

Two Cooks per Company will go with this lorry and prepare dinners for Battalion on arrival.

Para 3.   Add :- Men taking part in Divisional Sports will leave their kits at Company Stores. Company Commanders will arrange to convey to Forest Camp.

Para. 4.   Area Stores:- All Area Stores will be collected into Mess Room of Companies, not "C" & "D" Companys' Mess Room. Paliasses will be stacked filled.

30/8/19.   (Sgd) F.W.Gilbert, Capt, & Adjt.
                                        10th. Bn. "Queens" R.W.S. Regt.

Copies to all recipients of O.O. 34.

1st. AMENDMENT TO OPERATION ORDER No. 34.
===

Para. 7.

    Add - Four Quartermasters Storemen
        One man from Canteen.
        One Officers' Mess Waiter.
        One Education Sergeant.

                                              (Sgd) F.W.Gilbert, Capt. & Adjt.
30/8/19.   10th. Bn. "Queens" R.W.S. Regt.

Copies to all recipients of O.O. 34.

Army Form C. 2118.

WAR DIARY
or
INTELLIGENCE SUMMARY.
(Erase heading not required.)

Instructions regarding War Diaries and Intelligence Summaries are contained in F.S. Regs., Part II. and the Staff Manual respectively. Title pages will be prepared in manuscript.

Place	Date	Hour	Summary of Events and Information	Remarks and references to Appendices
Forest Camp SEIGBURG Germany	1/9/19		Batt. relieved Guards of 57th Bn Hampshire Regt in Siegburg and LIND. HQrs and "A" & "C" Coys to FOREST CAMP.	C.H. Barge Lt Col Comdg (R.W.S.) Regt
"	2/9/19		"B"Coy carried out Guard Duties over Army Ammunition Dump and Technical College Siegburg. "B" Coy. at LIND was relieved by 19th Bn Middx Regt and came in to FOREST CAMP. A Coy commenced Firing General Musketry Course in SEIGBURG RANGE. C Coy found Range Parties.	
"	3/9/19		"A"Coy continued firing G.M.C. "C" Coy found Range Parties. "B" Coy carried out Guard duties as above. B Coy carried out Company Training and Education.	
"	4/9/19		Same in all cases as for Sept 3rd	
"	5/9/19		"A" Coy completed G.M.C. remainder as above for Sept 3rd	
"	6/9/19		"C" Coy commenced firing G.M.C. "A" Coy found Range Parties. B Coy carried out Interior Economy.	
"	7/9/19		D Coy Guard duties Siegburg. B of E Divine Service in Siegburg. R.C. Holy Mass LOHMAR CHURCH 10.30. Church Parades B of E 11.30hrs	

WAR DIARY
or
INTELLIGENCE SUMMARY.
(Erase heading not required.)

Army Form C. 2118.

Instructions regarding War Diaries and Intelligence Summaries are contained in F.S. Regs., Part II. and the Staff Manual respectively. Title pages will be prepared in manuscript.

Place	Date	Hour	Summary of Events and Information	Remarks and references to Appendices
FOREST CAMP SEIGBURG	8/9/19		"C" Company continued firing G.M.C. "A" Coy found Range Parties. Bn. Education. B Coy Guards Seigburg	
"	9/9/19		"C" Company completed firing G.M.C. A Coy Range parties "B" Coy training. "D" Guard duties	
"	10/9/19		"C" Coy finished firing G.M.C. "A" found Range Parties. "B" Coy sent Coy training. "D" Guards duties. Hay	
"	11/9/19		"B" Coy commenced firing G.M.C. "A" found Range Parties found by "B" Coy on Sergeants retired and Guard previously found by them on deploying C Coy relieved D Coy Shours as D Coy "B" Coy found Range Parties.	
"	12/9/19		"B" Coy continued G.M.C. "D" Coy found Range Parties. "A" Coy continued training. "C" Guard duties.	
"	13/9/19		B Coy continued firing G.M.C. D Coy found Range Parties. "A" kit inspection by C.O. Party returned from Army Rifle meeting having won the Cup for Lewis Gun Team Competition. C Coy Guard duties	
"	14/9/19		Church Parades. C of E Divine service 11.30 hrs Roman Catholic LOHMAR CHURCH 10.30 hrs	

Army Form C. 2118.

WAR DIARY
or
INTELLIGENCE SUMMARY.
(Erase heading not required.)

Instructions regarding War Diaries and Intelligence Summaries are contained in F. S. Regs., Part II. and the Staff Manual respectively. Title pages will be prepared in manuscript.

Place	Date	Hour	Summary of Events and Information	Remarks and references to Appendices
To rest Camp Seigburg	15/9/19		B Coy continued firing G.M.C. O Coy found Range Parties. A Coy carried out Company Training. C Coy Guard Duties	Pte H 1st Queens (R.A.C.) 13t [signature]
"	16/9/19		Whole Regiment at a Holiday on account of Divisional Show.	
"	17/9/19		B Coy continued G.M.C. A Coy found Range Parties. D Coy concentrated on preliminary musketry before firing G.M.C. C Coy Guard duties Seigburg	
"	18/9/19		B Coy completed G.M.C. A Coy found Range Parties. D Coy musketry. C Coy Guard Duties SEIGBURG.	
"	19/9/19		D Coy commenced firing G.M.C. B Coy found Range Duties. C Coy Guard duties. A Coy Education 09.00 – 11.00 hrs Coy Training in morning.	
"	20/9/19		D Coy continued G.M.C. B Coy found Range parties. A Coy carried out Interior economy. C Coy Guard duties SEIGBURG. Church Parades. C of E. Divine Service in Canteen at 09.30 hrs. R.C. Holy Mass 09.30 LOHMAR CHURCH. A B + D Coys attended. Morning Service 09.30 hrs. Non-Conformist.	
"	22/9/19		Camp Inspection by G.O 10.30 to 11.30 hrs. D Coy continued G.M.C. B Coy found Range Parties. C Coy Guard duties SEIGBURG. A Coy Company training 09.30 – 12.45 hr.	

Army Form C. 2118.

WAR DIARY
or
INTELLIGENCE SUMMARY.
(Erase heading not required.)

Instructions regarding War Diaries and Intelligence Summaries are contained in F. S. Regs., Part II. and the Staff Manual respectively. Title pages will be prepared in manuscript.

Place	Date	Hour	Summary of Events and Information	Remarks and references to Appendices
FOREST CAMP	23/9/19		D. Coy. continued firing G.M.C. B. Coy. found Range Parties. C. Coy. carried out Guard duties. A Coy. Education from 09.30-12.45.	
SEIGBURG	24/9/19		D. Coy continued firing G.M.C. Men of A & B Coys who had not fired G.M.C. carried out musketry from 09.00-12.30. Remaining men of these Coys found Range Parties. C. Coy. were relieved from Guard Duties SEIGBURG by 2/4th Bn. "Queens", and returned to camp.	
"	25/9/19		D. Coy. completed Firing G.M.C. Bath. details carried out musketry from 09.00 to 12.30 hrs. The G.O.C. inspected kits of C. Coy.	
"	26/9/19		Bath. details for G.M.C. carried out musketry. Remainder carried out Education and Company Training.	
"	27/9/19		Bath. details commenced firing G.M.C. Remaining men of A & C Coys. found Range duties. Remaining men of B & D Education and Interior Economy.	
"	28/9/19		Church Parade. C of E Divine Service 09.30 hrs. R.C. Holy Mass 09.30. Non-conformist morning service 09.30 hrs.	
"	29/9/19		Bath. details continued firing G.M.C. Remaining men of D. Coy. found Range Parties. Remainder of A & C Coys carried out Company Training.	
"	30/9/19		Bath. details continued G.M.C. firing. Remainder of D Coy found Company Training Parties. Remainder of A & C were employed on working Party & Range parties.	

41ST DIVISION
123RD INFY BDE

11TH BN QUEEN'S R.W.SURREYS
MAY 1916-DEC 1918 (OCT 91)
MAR 1918 — 1919 SEP

TO RHINE BDE
RHINE GARRISON

IN ITALY 1917 NOV — 1918 FEB

Box 2638